Firefighters and Support Members,

The past twelve months has flashed by in the blink of an eye. This book chronicles that period of time - between October 2015 to October 2016.

This book chronicles emergency responses, fire prevention, training, mentoring, maintenance of trucks and fire hydrants, building inspections, and the list goes on.

Whether it be a fire, a rescue, or a medical assist. As a fire department, I believe we accomplish more than any department our size.

Our City of El Dorado team – fellow city departments, city manager, city council citizens – it takes us all. What we did as a fire department wouldn't have been possible without the whole team.

Firefighters, I personally applaud your effort as I know the Citizens of El Dorado do. I hope you and others enjoy this book.

Sincerely,
Steve Moody
El Dorado Fire Chief

Hands On The Wall

On many things there are "hands on the wall" that go unrecognized. The many portrait frames in the fire stations were all built by members of the correctional facility. Unfortunately, we cannot identify them by name or face. Only by hands

EARLY MORNING – Combine Fire

El Dorado Fire was paged to a combine on fire in the area of Bluestem and SE 20th early Friday morning. The combine involved in the fire was a total loss and a semi-truck and trailer parked nearby sustained some heat damage.

The cause of the fire was undetermined after investigation.

Texas A&M Engineering Extension Service (TEEX) – College Station, Texas

"Every participant should complete this fire school with the knowledge, understanding, and demonstrate proficient ability to safely execute live fire training scenarios addressing the following elements: Incident Command; Tactics & Strategy; Master Streams; Hose Streams, Hydraulics; Foam Application; Extinguishing Agents; SCBA Use.

That was on the front page of the program for the fire training that Lieutenant Shane McCoy and Master Firefighter Mike Rose attended at College Station, Texas this past week.

One side of each training book page listed on the left side what would be learned and on the right side what they called "take home points". The instructors were seven refinery Fire Chiefs from all across the nation.

Here is the full story of the training told by Master FF Mike Rose: El Dorado Firefighters were able to experience another dimension of firefighting this past week. Lieutenant Shane McCoy and Master Firefighter Mike Rose had the opportunity of a life time this past week and it was all made possible by the Holly Frontier Corporation. Holly Frontier invited two firefighters from the El Dorado Fire Department to participate in their Corporate Fire School at Texas A&M University in College Station, Texas. The long 9 hour dry to College Station was the easiest and most boring part of the adventure. After arriving, on

Monday evening, we met up with six guys from the El Dorado Refinery and 54 guys from other Holly Refineries. These gentleman traveled from Wyoming, New Mexico, Utah and several other states with one particular goal in mind. The goal was to learn more about Refinery firefighting and to improve your essential skills. As everyone set down to dinner, it reminded me of Holidays with my family. Everyone was talking, joking and laughing and the unique part of the whole situation was that we just met less than 2 hours before dinner. As I was lying on my bed, I had feelings of anxiety, self-doubt and wandering what was I doing at a place like this, or am I going to embarrass myself tomorrow at the training facility. What do I know about refinery firefighting?

Tuesday, 7 a.m comes early and as we set in the room to discuss the daily itinerary, I noticed that Shane and I weren't alone, we had brothers from other municipal departments from around the country. The Holly Fire Chiefs divided the group into two teams and my self-confidence went into the toilet. Shane and I have known each other for a while and now we found  ourselves on different teams with people we didn't know. I know this doesn't sound like much, but in the firefighting world, you trust your co-workers like a child trusts his parents. Shane knows what my skill level is and I know the exact same things about Shane.

So, in other words, I felt like a school age kid on his first day of kindergarten, not knowing what to expect. We approached the first prop, a bunch of pipes, valves, stairway to a second story and a couple racks of fire hose. No big deal, we assembled hose line teams and I was put in charge of handling the nozzle for the first training evolution. Wow, you can only imagine the thoughts that crossed my mind and then they ignited the propane prop which also had flammable liquid similar to gasoline. A seasoned veteran was right behind me and assured me that everything was going to be ok. Structural firefighting is so different and I was about to find out why in less than 30 minutes. In structural firefighting, we extinguish the fire using water in a rapid manner. In Industrial firefighting, we manipulate the fire with hose streams, meaning push the fire in a desired direction, and take the fuel from the fire by turning off a valve. No fuel for the fire to burn, means no more fire. We approached the first valve with a wide fog pattern and pushed the fire away from the valve and the nozzle ended up only inches away from the valve handle. The team leader turned the valve off and we backed away from the fire.

You would be working on extinguishing the fire on these props and what seemed only like 15 minutes, in reality was 1 hour and 15 minutes and you were exhausted. On Tuesday alone, it seemed like we shut down 100 valves with fire impinging on each valve and a fine water mist covered my face mask, impairing my vision. Each training prop became more difficult than the next and offered new challenges, that neither Shane or I had experienced before.

Wednesday, same as Tuesday, or at least I thought it was going to be close. If I could describe Wednesday in one word, it would be Foam. We learned about the capabilities and inabilities of foam. We applied foam to all different kinds of fuel fires, some were leaking from tank cars, trucks and fuel storage tanks. A foam blanket covers the fire and smothers the oxygen from the fire, extinguishing the fire. A small hole in a foam blanket caused by an extinguisher or nozzle can have life threatening consequences, so caution had to be used when operating firefighting equipment. Just like Tuesday, we were on the training grounds at 7 a.m. and finished fighting fire around 4:30 p.m. Eight hours of being in full gear, SCBA and the weather was a wonderful 80 degrees. Days like this, remind you of why you chose this profession.

Thursday, was a true test of courage and character. We started the day off at 5 a.m. on the training grounds and ready to prove to the instructors that we were capable of completing any job that was assigned. Firefighting is strenuous job and even the simplest task can become almost impossible to achieve, but add the fact that it is pitch black outside, now you have taken the job to the next level. You rely on sensation more than sight and the black valve that was easily seen during the day, is hidden in the shadows of over turned rail cars. The bright orange flames become distractive, lighting up the sky but the fuel valve As daylight approaches, you realize that the training prop was simple to operate but the night time darkness impaired your vision just enough to make the operation seem impossible.

Team work, encouragement and guidance from Instructors, team members, co-workers and friends made the impossible feat a reality. The last challenge was for us to assemble team member to attack a huge amount of fire on what seemed to be a single prop. Sixty firefighters working against the clock to beat impossible odds as the Instructors stood by and evaluated our performance. Just as the last fire was extinguished, another prop would ignite and the process would start all over again. So, remember at the first, I said it took 1 hour and 15 minutes to extinguish one prop on the first day, we extinguished 3 props within an hour and the fire was more intense than anything we encountered on the first day.

This experience gave Shane and I the knowledge, skills, courage and drive to become better firefighters. Most importantly, it helps us better serve the citizens of El Dorado, and the employees of Holly Frontier Refinery. Friendships were built, memories were made and a new love for this job was all acquired in four days of training. I would like to say "Thank You" to Holly Frontier Refinery, Fire Chief Moody, Captain Max Brown and the City of El Dorado for allowing me to attend this wonderful training at Texas A&M University. I encourage all firefighters, young and old to attend any training offered at TEEX. It was a whirlwind trip. The two got back at 1:00 am this morning. Holly Frontier paid for all of both Mike and Shane's expenses. An expense that otherwise wouldn't have been doable. The "take home points" were many And Mike said, "The training was incredible. Easily the best he has ever attended."

Hometown Heroes – Getting To Know Your Firefighters

Chief Moody began with the El Dorado Fire Department in October of 2013. Steve began his adventure in the fire service as a firefighter with Salina Fire Department in 1978. He worked up through the ranks and served as Deputy Chief from 1996 until his departure in 2006. Steve then went on to be the Fire Chief for the Leavenworth Fire Department from 2006 until 2009. In 2009 Steve moved west to become the Emergency Service Director for Stafford County until 2013.

Chief Moody was born and raised in Salina Kansas. After graduating from Salina Central High School Chief attended Hutchinson Community College completing an Associates of Applied Science Degree in Emergency Medical Services, where he obtained his Paramedic certification. Chief Moody continued his education attending K-State completing a Bachelor's Degree in Technology Management in 2001. Chief Moody is also a Certified Public Manager, Certified Emergency Manager, and has completed the National Fire Academy's Executive Fire Officer Program. Chief Moody married his high school sweetheart, Rosie. They have been married for 37 years but together for 42 years. They have two sons Matthew and Weston. Their oldest, Matthew is married to his wife Erin and they have two children Macoy and Vienna. Weston, the youngest is married to his wife Kiely and they have two children as well, Amaia and Grayson. Chief Moody, while very involved with various emergency service organizations and committees, he likes to spend his down time visiting his children and spending time with his grandchildren. In his spare time Chief likes to do carpentry work and welding.

Chief recalled one of the memorable moments in the fire service being a fire at the St. Johns Academy in Salina. At this particular fire he had the opportunity to climb a Bangor Ladder, which is a 50ft. ladder that uses stay-poles to stabilize it when extended because of its great height. He also recalled how they made an aggressive fire attack only to find that there was a common attic that contributed to the rapid fire growth. The crews

eventually had to back out and go defensive. All that excitement and it was only his first week on the Salina Fire Department!

Chief describes one of his greatest career accomplishments as being able to be successful in four different agencies; Salina, Leavenworth, Stafford County and El Dorado Fire Departments. Another great accomplishment Chief recalled is the completion of the Executive Fire Officer Program through the National Fire Academy. One of the most challenging aspects of his career is working with the three groups here within the El Dorado Fire Department; the paid officers, the volunteers/ reserves, and the students. Thank you Chief for all you do!

DRIVER OPERATOR – David Wilson

David Wilson is one our most tenured Volunteers. A while back a decision was made to widen the scope of our volunteers to include squad truck driving. David passed the written test part of the process. Once he completes the hands on portion then he'll be good to go as a driver. Congratulations David!

WILD LAND FIRE – Multiple Department Response

Kansas wild land fires that are wind aided can move rapidly, and that was the case late this morning with a fire on Shumway, midway between 50th and 40th in Butler County. Trucks from nine different departments, twenty trucks with firefighters, fought the fire. Several homes were in close proximity to the fire, but thanks to firefighting efforts, none incurred any damage. Personnel were on scene over an hour and a half. No cause for the fire has been determined.

AUTO ACCIDENT – Pine & Star

There was a two vehicle accident this morning at Pine & Star. The accident caused significant vehicle damages and minor injury to one.

Police, Fire and EMS responded to the accident.

WILDLAND FIRE – 50th and Teeter

El Dorado Fire was dispatched mid-morning on a large grassland fire at SE 50th and Teeter Road. The fire was approximately 30 acres in size. Assistance was requested from and received from Leon. Firefighters were on scene several hours extinguishing hotspots in the grass and putting out burning trees. Conditions are prime for grassland fires. Anybody conducting operations of any kind off road need to take extra

TOWANDA FIRE – **Mutual Aide**

El Dorado firefighters helped Towanda with a grassland fire early this afternoon.

The fire burned approximately 40 acres. Ravines and old protruding pipes presented additional dangers.

The fire was controlled after approximately one hour

CHLORINE – Hazmat Training

Members of the El Dorado Fire Department participated in a mock chlorine leak scenario this morning. The place was of the exercise was the water treatment plant. Firefighters started by taking command of the incident. There was a report of a worker down just inside the front door. Two firefighters dressed in turnout gear and breathing air packs to effect the rescue of the worker. After the worker was rescued it was time to stop the leak .Two more firefighters dressed in full Level A hazmat suits. The firefighters took a special kit to cap off the leaking cylinder. Dispatch and Emergency Management personnel all participated in the event. Afterwards, the group met at the fire station to debrief on lessons learned. Great job by all.

FIREFIGHTERS & POLITICIANS – How Do They Compare?

One does the job as a civic duty with no personal gain – the other receives a big personal gain. One receives little to no compensation – the other receives a nice wage with a lifetime pension. One spends nothing to get elected – the other spends a fortune. One has goals to save property and lives – the other has monetary goals for a select few. One risks life to do the job – the other goes to meetings.

Is it any wonder that we trust one a bit more than the other? *Whatever party you side on, be sure the person you are supporting will support the good of the citizens they serve.

Christmas Time – People Helping People -

It's that time of year again. Gifts beneath the tree. Tasty food on the stove. But not for everyone And that is why the Salvation Army collects gifts and food for those that would have nothing otherwise. Today, El Dorado firefighters helped box toys and canned goods. The many people who donated items are mighty special.

A big Thank You to all.

Structure Fire – Lowe Street

Firefighters are on the scene of a bedroom fire. The fire was brought under control quickly.

Damage to the home is unknown and the cause of the fire is undetermined at this time

.

K-12 SAW – A Benevolent Businessman

His name is Robbie Pollard. Pollard is a self-employed electrician and a benevolent one too.

He came into the fire station a week or so ago – said he had a very good year of business and wanted to give back to the community. What he proposed was to donate a K-12 Saw to the department. He knew the department didn't own one. Pollard has a special knowledge of the fire department because his son was an El Dorado Fire Department firefighter. Donating a saw is pretty special. The K12 saw can cut just about anything including concrete. It could someday mean the difference between life and death. If you see Mr. Pollard, be sure and thank him

El Dorado Christmas Parade

A good crowd was downtown this evening. The reason was the annual Christmas parade.

El Dorado firefighters spent the afternoon hanging lights from two of their trucks as their part in the parade.

An honor guard led the way and towards the end of the parade was Ole Santa Clause and Mrs. Clause. Be sure and be good because there's just 21 days until Christmas!

Structure Fire – Heavy Damage

A fire in a home on E. 29th Street caused extensive damage. The occupant awakened to heavy smoke. She made her way into the

living room area and found a large amount of fire in the corner of the room where a Christmas tree was located. Firefighters made a quick stop of the fire, but the living room was a total loss. Likewise, the entire home suffered smoke and heat damage. The fire cause is undetermined at this time. However, the seat of the fire was in the vicinity of the Christmas tree. There was just the one person home and she escaped without injury

AUTO ACCIDENT – Emporia & Fourth

Early this afternoon emergency personnel worked a two-vehicle accident at the intersection of Emporia and W. 4th

The intersection is an open intersection with no signage.

None of the passengers were injured.

Helmet Cam Video: Haverhill Rd

The video showed the incredible job firefighters did in saving a home yesterday afternoon. The breezeway between the two structures had major fire damage, but the home only suffered minor heat damage.

This fire was fed from a 50 gallon gasoline tank located in the metal structure. Firefighters stayed on scene throughout the night tending to rekindles. The metal building and its contents was a total loss. The cause of the fire has not been determined

HAZMAT Demonstration

The LEPC Local Emergency Preparedness Committee conducted their regularly scheduled meeting this afternoon at BG Products. Captain Troy Jellison, Master FF Derick Boggs, and Master FF Caleb Carson gave a demonstration to the group.

They brought a small chemical sample to test whether the product had flammable off-gas, whether it was flammable, whether it was miscible with water, and whether it was corrosive. After these tests the group was told what the chemical was – floor cleaner.

El Dorado FD responds to hazardous material calls throughout Butler County through a county/city agreement. If things get complicated the Regional team from Wichita can be called.

Congratulation Chris Brown

El Dorado Fire Department Firefighter Chris Brown has successfully passed his Firefighter 1 certification. Chris has been with the department for some time as a firefighter, but just hadn't finished everything for the Firefighter 1 certification.

Congratulations!

Captain Max Brown – Retirement

Friends, family, and cohorts gathered at the City Commission chambers Friday afternoon from 3-5 pm to honor Captain Max Brown.

Max started his service back when the police and fire were combined as Public Safety. He has seen a lot of change during his tenure.

We wish Max the very best in retirement.

Promotions – Jack, Mike, & Quentin

Jack Zimmerman, Michael Rose, and Quentin Sage. These were the three El Dorado firefighters who received promotions this evening.

It was the official "Badge Pinning" ceremony.

Jack was promoted to Captain, Michael was promoted to Lieutenant, and Quentin was promoted to Master Firefighter.

Family, friends, and co-workers came to watch the badge pinning. Jack and Quentin had their fathers pin them and Michael had his wife do the honors.

The three read the department's Pride in Service pledge before being pinned. Afterwards, there was cake and punch served.

Congratulations gentlemen!

Welcome Back Chris

Chris McGathy returned to the El Dorado Fire Department.

His first day was August 2nd. He was assigned shift 1.

Welcome back Chris

Monster Wild Land Fire

Firefighters from seven different departments fought a grassland fire that covered up to four miles in length. Fire trucks totaled over twenty and firefighters over forty. It's unknown what started the fire, but the dryness, heat and winds were the ingredients of a monster fire. Large open grounds without roadways kept any natural stop points to help aid firefighters. Simultaneously, firefighters in Butler County fought several other fires. Virtually every fire department in the county was involved in a firefight. Firefighters worked over three hours fighting the fire. At this same time

firefighters and EMS worked two serious auto accidents that occurred on the turnpike.

Hometown Heroes – Getting to Know Your Firefighters

This month's Hometown Hero is Chad Wittenberg. Chad is someone you don't see a lot of, but his work on scene is very evident. Without his contribution much of our stories cannot be told. While he may not be found dragging fire hose to the front door, laddering the roof of the blazing building, or popping the door of a mangled car on the highway, you can bet he will be right in the action with camera in hand! You see, Chad's role is to capture all the images that tell the story of what our guys do. Without his awesome shots our stories will only be heard by word of mouth at the coffee shop or read in the headlines of the next day's newspaper.

What Chad provides not only brings a great sense of pride to the department, but an opportunity for the community to see that the fire service is very challenging and the situations our guys face are not for the faint of heart. Chad was born in Kansas City, Kansas . He attended El Dorado High School and graduated in 1986. After High School Chad went on to Butler Community College where he majored in Biology. After graduating from Butler he went Emporia State University majoring in Environmental Biology.

Chad is married to Dr. Beth Wittenberg and they have three boys together; Cody, Zach, and Levi. Chad and Beth met while they were attending Emporia State University. Dr. Beth owns and operates the Natural Pet Care Center located in El Dorado. Their children attend El Dorado schools and are very active in sports. Chad

could not really recall a time when he didn't have a camera with him. While in college he would take shots of the weather and wildlife. He sold the pictures to the Biology Departments. Chad is a jack of all trades, during the summer time he does a lot of professional photo shoots. He has been known to do a couple concrete jobs here and there. He even helps out at his wife's business. When not chasing fire trucks Chad enjoys spending time with his family. Chad enjoys being behind the lens and capturing all that nature has to offer. He and his wife spend many hours following their three boys to all the various sporting events they are involved in. When time allows Chad enjoys fishing with the boys.

Chad began capturing shots of our department one day when he was called in to Chief Moody's office. Chief had seen Chads work and wanted to know if he would be willing to capture those moments on a regular basis. Chief Moody outfitted Chad with a pager, so he would know when and where the photo opportunities came about and Chad was given an official department ID and shirt granting him access to the departments incidents.

You can see from the galleries of action shots, Chad is not some fly by night action junkie that enjoys taking pictures of peoples worse moments, but yet he captures ordinary men accomplishing extra ordinary task, and he does so with class and respect. Many of the pictures used in the department's blog are those captured by Chad. Thank you Chad for sharing our world through your lens. We look forward to many more pictures! So the next time you read the blog or see a guy at the emergency scene wearing an El Dorado Fire shirt with camera in hand, that's Chad!

Famous Chad

Chad is famous! The El Dorado Fire Department and friends thereof aren't the only ones who appreciate his fine work. The State Fire Marshal's office is using this Chad photo as a  header for their Facebook and Twitter accounts. This was the photo of the fire that had 9 departments respond to. Thank you Chad and Thank you Sara with the State FM Office.

Smoke Detector Program

Eldorado Lieutenant Coby Spear recently attended the National Fire Academy and came back with a wonderful idea. The El Dorado Fire Department is teaming up with the American Red Cross to provide smoke detectors – free of charge – to any El Dorado citizen.

The entire city will be canvassed. The detectors being installed are the 10 year model. No battery needs replaced. The detector simply runs a 10 year cycle whereby it's replaced at the end of 10 years.

Give us a call if you would like to jump to the front of the pack.

Mobile Home Fire

The deck on the front of the home was ablaze upon firefighter's arrival. The area completely surrounding the home was burned too.
Firefighters made a quick attack on the fire, but not before it had extended to the underside of the home. The fire also extended into the interior.

Firefighters performed a major amount of overhaul to extinguish the entirety of the fire.

The cause of the fire is under investigation

Fire Prevention

One of the many things we do as firefighters is talking with kids about fire safety. Throughout the year we try to get to all the daycares in town to talk to the kids and show them the equipment we use to do our job.

On Tuesday February 2nd, we talked to 20 preschoolers at El Dorado Head Start, telling them not to hide in their house if it is on fire and about what a firefighter looks like in his fire gear and not to be afraid if they see us like this.

Seeing what we look like in our gear and seeing that we are not scary before there is an emergency hopefully will trigger that memory in an emergency. After a short talk from Captain Jack Zimmerman and watching Student Resident Ethan Herrick get in his fire gear the students went outside in the cold weather to look at the fire truck.

Master Firefighter Derick Boggs was outside to show the kids the truck. This is just one of many ways that we serve our community to make it a better place to live.

NFPA TRIP

The National Fire Academy's (NFA's) Managing Officer Program is a  multiyear curriculum that introduces emerging emergency services leaders to personal and professional skills in change management, risk reduction and adaptive leadership. Acceptance into the program is the first step in your professional development as a career or volunteer fire/Emergency Medical Services (EMS) manager, and includes all four elements of professional development: education, training, experience and continuing education.

The Managing Officer Program will build on foundational management and technical competencies, learning to address issues of interpersonal and cultural sensitivity, professional ethics, and outcome-based performance. On completion of the program, Lieutenant Spear will:

Be better prepared to grow professionally, improve their skills, and meet emerging professional challenges.

Be able to embrace professional growth and development in their career.

Enjoy a national perspective on professional development.

Understand and appreciate the importance of professional development.

Have a network of fire service professionals who support career development.

"We are proud to support Lieutenant Spear his efforts to better protect the citizens of El Dorado. "The National Fire Academy provides unparalleled continuing education and we look forward to implementing this advance officer training into all our department activities."

The National Fire Academy was created as a result of the landmark document America Burning and the subsequent passage of the Federal Fire Prevention and Control Act of 1974. It is estimated that, since 1975, over 1,400,000 students have received training through a variety of course delivery methods. Countless lives have been saved and property losses prevented as a direct result of this training and education.

Badge Pinning Ceremony

A good crowd of firefighters attended the event. It was a Badge Pinning ceremony.

The two firefighters are the newest members of the El Dorado Fire Department. Ben comes to us from Wichita. He went through the Butler Community College Fire Science program and has family in the Wichita area.

LJ comes to us from Oklahoma. His training has been through the Oklahoma State Fire program. LJ is married with two children. His wife's name is April and his children Haley and Porter. Before having their badges pinned each firefighter recited the El Dorado Pledge of Service. Then it was time for the badge pinning. Ben's captain pinned his badge and LJ's wife April pinned his.

After the badge pinning each firefighter was given a St. Florian (Patron Saint of Firefighters) coin with a hand shake from Chief Moody.

Welcome aboard!

Five Fires in a Row

The first one was on 4th Street Terrace and was caused by a piece of metal roofing blowing against an electrical line. Sparks fell to the ground and lit the grass on fire. It quickly spread to a wooden fence endangering two homes. A resident suffered second degree burns to all his fingers on one hand. Just as firefighters were getting this fire under control, another fire occurred. This fire was located at the land fill. The fire got into a tree belt. A bull dozer had to be used to push a large hollow tree into a creek bed. Chain saws were also brought into action. While still on this fire on came fire number three. Fire number three was a rekindle of a fire fought by crews days before. A large pile of logs was afire stoked by the harsh wind. Firefighters had to drag some of the extra large logs into a burned out area. While on this fire a request for mutual aid was received from White Water. El Dorado sent two squads to that fire. That was fire four. Then came fire number five. And it proved to be the biggest. The fire was located on 40th Street and Haverhill. The fire was in the Burns district, but a mutual aid request for El Dorado and others was dispatched. This fire took close to three hours to control. The haze in the sky could be seen miles away. Five fires in a row. A great job of firefighting.

Motor Home

Firefighters got the fire in the 2100 Block of US 54 under control in short order, but the motorhome fire was discovered too late to save it. Literally, there was only a framework left of the motorhome when firefighters arrived on scene. Firefighters extinguished the core fire within several minutes, but stayed on scene for another thirty minutes putting out hot spots. Cause of the fire is unknown at this time.

Patch Collection

Retired El Dorado Inspector Jerry Urton spent a career collecting them. Fire department patches. The inmates made some beautiful display cases. They are hanging up at fire station 2. Stop by and see them if you get the chance

Wildland Fires Take Toll On Local Crews

Jade DeGood, jdegood@kwch.com

Butler County, Kan -

Strong winds, tall grass and little moisture have led to the perfect storm for wildland fires this years. "The wind, of course, is what fuels the wildland fires to a degree that it makes it difficult to put them out," said Chief Moody of the El Dorado Fire Department. We've been busy. It's the time of the year to burn and yet, when the winds blow like they do it's hard to keep it under control and likely, many get out of control."Spring in Kansas has meant long days for local fire crews. "It's been pretty hectic," said Samuel Aitchison, an El Dorado Firefighter. "People have these controlled burns the day before the wind picks up and they don't get it all the way out, which is hectic for us because it causes the embers to blow into the unburned area in the trees." The El Dorado Fire Department went to 15 wildland fires in just 24 hours Tuesday.

"Over all it was a long day," said Samuel Wheeler, another El Dorado Firefighter. "Our guys got done around 2 o'clock in the morning." Those long hours have been all too common for many firefighters in Kansas this March and April.

"It's kind of difficult with us because our staffing is so thin, we're using everybody," said Chief Moody. "We only run five guys out of El Dorado, so we rely on the volunteers," said Aitchison.

"Usually the guy on the front is pretty exhausted from fighting up there, or cutting fence, or just doing overall work in general on the fire," said Wheeler. Wind gusts of 30, 40 and 50 miles-per-hour have worked against fire crews, spreading embers quicker than they are extinguished.

"Fifteen calls ads up to quite a few hours," said Chief Moody. "It pretty much is a day without sleep and pretty much you've been fighting them all night long."

But the long hours, rigorous work and sometimes rugged terrain is exactly what these firefighters knew they were signing up for.

"Just the satisfaction of being able to change people's lives," said Aitchison. "It's not just helping people, it's knowing that it's someone's property and seeing the smiles on their face when we get doe."

NFA Executive Fire Officer Program

The National Fire Academy Executive Fire Officer program. It's the flagship program for the NFA and our very own Captain Troy Jellison is attending.

He reports that the course is tough. And this is but one of the four trips he will make to conclude the program. With research papers required post each class conclusion.

Congratulations on being chosen!

Training Tower

You can do training without one., but ISO Insurance Service Organization gives you points towards your fire rating if you have one, and it makes training a lot safer. That thing is a training tower.

Yesterday morning the crane was lifting the training pods onto their spots. Because of anticipated high winds the top pod wasn't lifted onto its' spot until today. The pod system has a number of features built into it. There's a door that can be forcibly opened. There's a gable roof section that allows firefighters to cut roofing holes. A burn room, a confined space prop, a sprinkler system, , a rappelling spot, and a stand pipe system. The training tower was made possible through a partnership between Butler Community College and the City of El Dorado. The college paid for the training tower itself and the city provided the land, the concrete support pods and drive pads, the placement of a fire hydrant, and the running of the electrical. The training tower will be an invaluable tool for years to come. Many people were instrumental in getting the training tower. A formal opening ceremony of the training tower will take place as soon as all the work is complete.

Electrical Fire

The dispatch came in as a "person on fire." Luckily, that wasn't what it was. The fire was an electrical one. Upon firefighter's arrival, the electrical wire had burned in two and was whipping across the ground. Fire was encircling the wall where the electrical panel was as well as the grass on the ground.

Firefighters stood by monitoring the situation until Weststar arrived to cut the power at the utility pole. Firefighters then did a thorough job of overhaul. Grass around the building was extinguished as well.

The wall around the electric panel was destroyed.

Tower #1 Christening

Whenever a fire department goes through the process of buying a new fire truck a committee from within the department visits the different plants. It's through those trips that the group  develops the specifications which must be met.

Afterwards is the bid letting.

The truck is then awarded to the manufacturer who meets the specifications and is overall the best choice.

During the building process members of the truck committee make two trips back to the plant to make sure specifications are being met. Once the truck is built and meets all specifications, it's delivered to the fire department.

That brings us to today.

The Tower 1 truck committee consisted of Captain Max Brown, Captain  Troy Jellison, Captain Jack Zimmerman, Lieutenant Shane McCoy, and Lieutenant Michael Rose. As you see the truck, the group clearly did a marvelous job. The crowd gave them a round of applause.

Serving at the time of Tower 1 being conceptualized was City Manager Herb Llewellyn, Mayor Michael Fagg, Commissioners Chase Locke, Nick Badwey, Bill Young, and David

Chapin, and Fire Chief Ken Nakaten. At the end of acquiring this vehicle was the addition of Mayor Vince Haines, Commissioners Gregg Lewis and Kendra Wilkinson. Without their support Tower 1 wouldn't have been possible. The crowd gave them a round of applause.

Dating back as far as one can look is the practice of christening a new fire truck. The very first fire trucks were horse drawn and many of the streets were dirt. As a matter of fact the City of El Dorado had two horses named Ned and Ted, which we have a custom made decal on Tower 1 depicting them.

Anyway, historically fire trucks are washed on the apron entrance before they are pulled into the fire station. Firefighters also have a long tradition of keeping their fire trucks polished clean. So, the trucks are washed before they are pulled back into the fire station after a call for service making them ready for call.

Children and some adults came forward and helped christen Tower 1 by washing it down.

Chief Moody asked for everyone's attention. He then asked everybody to bow their heads while he said the blessing for Tower 1.

Bless This Truck

Lord, the emergencies they will be many.

Often times this truck and those who ride it will be in harm's way.

Father, Bless this Truck and the men and women who man it.

Protect it and protect them while they protect others.

All this we ask humbly of you.

Amen

Mayor Vince Haines did the honors of the "cutting of the tape?" Afterwards, retired Captain and truck committee chair, Max Brown, officially sounded the sirens as he backed into the fire station. He then radioed Dispatch putting the truck into official service with the following message: *"Dispatch, this is El Dorado Tower 1. Please officially place Tower 1 in service."*

A number of people then helped dry the truck.

Tower 1 will have a long, safe, successful life with the El Dorado Fire Department. The event concluded with thanks to everyone for coming out for the truck christening.

Ladder Training

Fire crews trained Tuesday evening on ladders. pecifically, training centered on the ladders on the new aerial truck.

Great training!

Grade School Fun Day

Fire crews made a trip to the local grade school today Fun dayfor their "fun day". The new ladder truck was a hit dropping water onto the children below. Summer will bring about many opportunities to enjoy the water at the local swimming pools.
Have a fun, safe summer.

House Fire SW 55th

The owner had been gone just a short time at the lumber yard. When he arrived home fire crews were fighting a fire in his home. The fire was confined to one bedroom, but totally consumed that area of the home. The bed in the room had an electronic control system It was undetermined if that or something else was the cause of the fire. Firefighters did a great job of keeping the fire confined to the one bedroom.

The Art of Firemanship Days

El Dorado firefighter Bryce Scott recently attended The Art of Firemanship Days in Harrisburg, Pennsylvania. The training was 3 days in length and covered topics such as engine company operations, search operations, ladders, ventilation, and how to reduce the risk of firefighters losing their lives in house fires.

Along with great training, Bryce was also able to learn drills to bring back and share with the department.

Relay Pumping

More and more home owners are building this way. Out in the country with a bit of acreage in the county down a long, narrow dirt roadway for a drive with no fire hydrant.

This presents a challenge for firefighters. Getting trucks down the narrow drive as well as turning them around to get back onto the roadway. So, firefighters from northern Butler County got together last evening to train on these kind of fires. The method practiced was for the first pumper that arrives on scene, (before driving down the driveway) drop a feeder hose at the driveway entrance.

The second pumper that arrives on scene places a "Y" connector on the end of the feeder. It is now a water supplier for the pumper. The "Y" has a clapper valve in it so either one or two pumpers can pump into the hose feeding the pumper at the house. The second truck on scene also hooks into the "Y". As one pumper finishes pumping its water it pulls away and another tanker takes the place of the first pumper, and so forth. The operation can continue on for as long as there is a pumper to feed the on scene pumper. Nobody has to go down the narrow roadway except the first pumper. Great training by all involved

Junior Firefighter Celebration

Butler County students were recognized for their achievement. The feat was the top score in the Junior Firefighter training.

Their hard work resulted in a pizza party. Ten pizzas were consumed, plus soda and cookies.

Congratulations on a special accomplishment and thank you Master Firefighter Caleb Carson for conducting the program.

College Station, Texas

Master Firefighters Derick Boggs and Quentin Sage have been in College Station, Texas this past week participating in refinery type firefighting. Derick and Quentin are participating in this training with fellow Holly Refinery firefighters

We will look forward to more photos when they get back home.

Hometown Hero's – Getting to Know Your Firefighters

This month's Hometown Hero spotlights Master Firefighter Caleb Carson.

Caleb was born in El Dorado and grew up just West of El Dorado. Caleb attended Circle High school in Towanda and graduated in 2010. After graduating Caleb decided to pursue a career in the fire service. Caleb attended Butler Community College where he took courses in Fire Science. During this time Caleb participated in Butler's Fire Science Residency Program with the El Dorado Fire Department, gaining the skills and knowledge to become a firefighter. Caleb took his first job as a Firefighter with the City of Atchison, Ks. There he worked as a Firefighter/ EMT until 2012. After his departure from Atchison, Ks. Caleb returned to the El Dorado area. In 2012 Caleb married Lindsey and they settled down and bought a house in El Dorado. They have two 4-legged children, Goliath and Ember.

Caleb began his career with the El Dorado Fire Department in 2012. He currently holds the position of Master Firefighter/ EMT and works out of Fire Station #1 located downtown. Some of Caleb's job responsibilities include driving the fire apparatus, and providing medical care, in addition to fighting fires. Another very important job duty Caleb has is conducting the Jr. Firefighter program for the 4th grade classes at the elementary schools in El Dorado. In this program Caleb delivers important safety

messages to the children, then at the end of the course those with the highest scores from each school get to embark on an adventure to the fire station for a pizza party.

On his days off from the working at the fire station Caleb runs his own lawn service, CC's Lawn Grooming. So you could say when Caleb is not taking care of the citizens in the community he is taking care of their yards!

Caleb enjoys doing projects around the house and taking to the water in his kayak.

When asked, what is the best aspect of your job in the fire service? Caleb replied. "Going to something different on every call. You never know what you're going to get called out to."

Caleb was also asked, what aspect of the fire service do you find most challenging? He replied, "It's not a bad thing. But adapting to the various personalities within the fire service."

Brad Sherry – Special Person/ Special Thanks

June 13, 2016

El Dorado Fire Department
Steve Moody, Fire Chief
220 East First Street
El Dorado, Kansas 67042

Dear Steve Moody;

Yesterday afternoon while traveling north on the Kansas Turnpike, a beep from somewhere within my dash board, told me that I was running low on fuel and that I needed to locate a service station and fill my gas tank. I exited the Kansas Turnpike and stopped at a Casey's Convenient Store. Well, I didn't know it when I entered the store with my purse and three small grand children towed behind me, but my life was about to be shaken.

When I reached for my wallet, it was missing! Quickly I remembered that I had left it in our "other" vehicle at our home 80 miles south of where I now stood. The reason I was traveling with my grandchildren was to pick up my husband, their grandfather, in the northeast corner of Kansas following his "Ride Across Kansas" bicycle tour. Now here the four of us stood TOTALLY STRANDED!!! I had no wallet, no ID, no cash or plastic, very little fuel and three small concerned grandchildren! The Casey's associate could not do anything to assist me, but beside me stood another customer named **Brad Sherry**. At first, he stood quietly nearby listening to my hard-luck story. I honestly wasn't aware that he was there. After the Casey's associate and I had conversed, **Brad Sherry** stepped up and towards me. He began to speak. He voiced that he could see I was in a dilemma with three little children close beside me and looks of concern on their small faces. He reached into his own pocket and pulled out his wallet. He proceeded to pay for my fuel. When I attempted to thank him or to get an address where by I could later re-pay him for his service he was doing for me at the time, he simply gently put out his hand as if to stop traffic and smiled toward both me and the children and said, "No thank you, but that will not be necessary. I am more than happy to assist you."

Now as I locate the address I am using at the top of this letter and your name and position, I write this little letter to acknowledge this American Hero, **Brad Sherry**. To the four of us, he was our biggest hero! The world needs more heroes like **Brad Sherry**.

Before we had driven out of El Dorado, two fire engines with sirens sounding, rumbled past us on the highway obviously going to the aid of others with problems in town. The children and I said a prayer to thank God for people such as these.

Thank you for having this hero on your fire staff. I feel safe and well protected with this man serving us in our time of need when he was off-duty but was willing to take of his personal time and resources to assist us when we needed it most.

Sincerely,

Anne Lassey
(316) 524-5028

Dog Bathing –

The Butler County Emergency Animal Response team is conducting their annual dog bathing fund raiser today. The event runs until 2pm at the El Dorado fire station on West 6th Street. The warm weather made the  experience as pleasurable as possible. It seemed the large dogs liked it best.   El Dorado firefighters helped with the dog washing. All the funds go to the Emergency Animal Response team. You still have a chance to make it if you hurry. Micro-chipping is also being offered.

Hope to see you

Verizon Back Pack Giveaway

Various businesses got together to put on a "backpack to school" event at Verizons this afternoon. Backpacks, notebooks, and pizza was given away. The fire department and Sheriff Herzet assisted with the event.

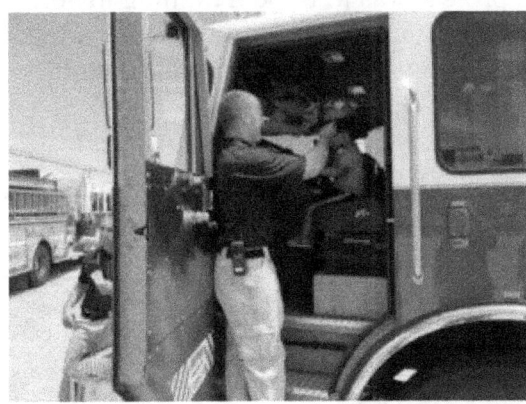

Training Tower Blessing

Today was the dedication of the new Training Tower. Several people spoke and then firefighters demonstrated the various uses of the training tower. Two sections of hose were uncoupled as a sign of the "opening" of the training tower. Below is Chief Moody's speech.

The Training Tower project got its beginning around three years ago as a request of mine and Captain Tony Yahghjian's for left-over sales tax funds. The dream project was to build a training tower. Our request was accepted by the sales tax committee. Afterwards, the funds sat idle until we could figure out how to acquire some additional funds needed.

From there it was the much grander vision of Captain Troy Jellison, Butler Community college Program Director Terry Love, and Chairman Anita Mills. They requested the college to pay the cost of the training tower itself – the actual building. The request was proposed and given the green light by the college board of trustees.

How it worked was the college paid the cost of the tower while the city paid for the property, concrete footings, concrete drives, electrical, and the placement of a fire hydrant.

So, here we are today giving our thanks. I applaud City Manager Herb Llewyln, the mayor, the commissioners, Dr. Krull, Annita Mills, and the Board of Trustees, for seeing the need of a tower without having its construction be a tragedy driven one.

Special thanks also goes out to Scott Rickard, Brad Meyer and Kurt Bookout and their men for the awesome work they did on the project – specifically all the concrete work and the placement of a fire hydrant.

The importance of this building is those who train with it are honing their lifesaving skills. It's kind of like a football team. You practice all week for the Sunday game knowing the team is only as good as they are practiced.

As we gather here today, it only seems right that the building be blessed. So, please join me with the

"Blessing of the Tower"

Lord, many will use this facility to train as emergency responders,

Any emergency operations training brings with it a certain amount of danger,

Father, we ask that you bless this facility and the men and women who use it.

Through the training provided may the emergency responders save lives and protect their own

All this we ask humbly of you.

Amen

Hometown Heroes – Getting to Know Your Firefighters

This month's Hometown Hero is L Jay Geist. L Jay was born and grew up in Scott City, Kansas. L Jay attended Scott City High School and graduated in 2001. After graduating, L Jay attended Hutchinson Community College. After College, he moved to Colorado to work for a landscaping company. While in Colorado he also worked as a professional bullfighter in rodeos.

In 2008 J Lay relocated from Colorado to Oklahoma, where he began his career in the fire service. L Jay joined the Hammond/ Elk City Fire Department and served as a Firefighter / Driver Operator. While attending college at Hutchinson Community College L Jay met the love of his live, April. The two would be married in 2008. They have two children; their son Porter, 7 years old and daughter Hillery who is 5 years old.

In 2016 L Jay joined the El Dorado Fire Department. He currently holds the position of and works on B Shift. L Jay is about to complete his 1 year probationary period and has proven to be a great asset to the department and the community.

L Jay likes to motive the guys on his crew to maintain peak physical fitness. Often times you can catch him in the mornings while on duty acting as the drill sergeant and running the guys on the crew through various different work out techniques and programs during physical fitness time. While it wears the guys out, they know the benefits!

On his days off from the fire station L Jay enjoys spending time with his family, taking in a game of golf with the guys and hunting. When asked, what is the best aspect of your job in the fire service? L Jay replied, "When I got hired on at Elk City. While you may not end up where you started, your first break is pretty cool!"

L Jay was also asked, what aspect of the fire service do you find most challenging? He replied, "Stressing the importance of physical fitness" (did you expected anything different from the drill sergeant.)Geist fitness In closing, L Jay was asked what advise he could give those looking to get into the fire service. His reply, "Do ride-a-longs, brush up on interview questions, and be humble."

L Jay, Thank you for your service to the community!

Rodney Reed Retirement

Rodney Reed. The name has a powerful ring to it. Most people only get a name as powerful as Rodney Reed by changing it – like an actor. Chief Moody remembers meeting Rodney when he came to a volunteer recognition event days from his first day with El Dorado. The event was at East Park. During that party a person was recognized as the volunteer of the year. It was a repeat performance bestowed upon Rodney.

Chief Moody told the crowd, "Now we are gathered here this evening to recognize Rodney for over 20 years of service to the citizens of El Dorado. During this time span Rodney has put out too many fires to remember them all." As much as any one item the firefighter helmet is a sign of the fire profession. Chief Moody presented Rodney with his fire helmet as a sign of appreciation.

Captain Jack Zimmerman was then asked to come forward to make the presentations from the firefighters. Firefighters gave Rodney an eight foot long oak board with two pieces of fire hose that each of the firefighters signed. Several other firefighters came forward and told some stories after which cake and punch was served. Rodney will be sorely missed.

Today It Was A Cell Phone

When somebody has a need for he lp and they can't think of

anybody else to help them, they call the fire department. And the requests can range widely. Today it was a cell phone.

The young man was having a jolly good time launching his phone up towards the ceiling at the YMCA. And then it happened – it alighted upon the floor joist and didn't come down.

The fire department was called. And, the crew quickly set and shimmied up the ladder to the rescue. Today it was a cell phone.

New Driver Operators

Sam Aitchson, Bryce Scott, and Sam Wheeler have officially passed their Driver Operator certification. Congratulations gentlemen.

K196 Motor Home Fire

The El Dorado and Towanda Fire Departments assisted the Potwin Fire Department with what was dispatched as a vehicle fire at NW 50th and Highway 196.

Upon arrival crews found a motor home fully engulfed with fire. The gasoline and the propane tank involvement hampered the fire fight. The roadway was closed down for approximately 45 minutes. Crews were able to extinguish the fire, but the motor home was a total loss. No injuries were sustained. The cause of the fire was undetermined.

Firefighter Zachary Floyd

El Dorado Volunteer Firefighter Zachary Floyd has accepted a full time position with the Wellington Fire Department. Zachary doesn't have his official starting date, but it will be soon. We appreciate the great job Zachary did for the El Dorado Fire Department. And we wish him the very best with Wellington.

Preventative Maintenance

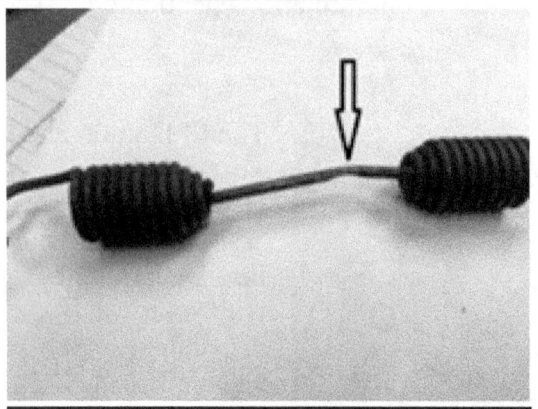

The Quint is a backup truck. The question is, "Should it be a lower priority for maintenance?" It was taken in for brake service. The mechanics found the spring on the wheel just about wore in two. It's hard to tell how long it would have been before failing.

If it would have failed it would've locked up the wheel. And it's hard to tell what would have happened after that. Never underestimate the importance of preventative maintenance. The answer to the question is "no" it should not be a lower priority.

El Dorado Firefighters MDA Fund

El Dorado Firefighters conducted their annual 2016 MDA fund drive at the local Dillons store. Citizens cleaned out their old change drawer and brought it out to help with the fund drive. A little over $4,000 was collected.

Sparky a.k.a. Lieutenant Coby Spear gave out hugs.

These girls cooked up 3 batches of brownies for the firefighters. They said with all that is going on in the country, they wanted to show us some appreciation for what the firefighters do. #PartofthePride

Rollover Auto Accident

El Dorado Fire, EMS, Law and County Rescue responded to a two vehicle auto accident at Emporia and 3rd Street late this afternoon. One patient suffered minor injuries and was transported by EMS

Wichita Stair Climb

The El Dorado Fire Department will be participating in the Wichita Memorial September 11th Stair Climb this Saturday, September 10th, 2016 at the Epic Center in the heart of Downtown Wichita.

The El Dorado Fire team will be represented by Lieutenant Shane McCoy, Lieutenant Coby Spear, Master Firefighter Derick Boggs, Firefighter Bryce Scott, Firefighter Sam Aitchison, Firefighter LJ Geist, Firefighter Scott VanPatten, and Firefighter Chris Towner.

Our team will be among many other fire departments climbing 110 stories to remember the 343 firefighters that lost their lives on that fateful day in 2001. Each firefighter will climb the 110 stories in full turn our gear and SCBA, weighing approximately 60 lbs. El Dorado Tower-1 will be flying the American Flag at the event to represent our community and city.

Oil Leak

A Kansas Highway Patrol trooper saw oil running down the ditch of the interstate highway just north of El Dorado. Fire crews responded and found what appeared to be an underground oil line rupture.

Firefighters also found that the oil ran down the ditch and into a creek. Oil line representatives were called and responded to the site with a backhoe. The oil representatives also shut down lines feeding the one leaking.

While the oil personnel were digging up the line with the backhoe, firefighters placed booms at several locations in the creek. Both the oil company and firefighters did a great job controlling the incident.

Camper Fire

El Dorado firefighters were paged to a structure fire early this afternoon. On arrival the firefighters found heavy smoke coming from a large 5th wheel camper. The camper was abandoned and empty. Firefighters made a quick entry and extinguished the fire. The investigation discovered that a young boy was playing with a lighter and caught a mattress on fire. The boy suffered some singed hair. Law enforcement was handling the situation with the boy.

May Day, May Day, May Day – Firefighter Down

Mayday, may day, may day – firefighter down!

That was the message conveyed to the volunteer firefighters who arrived on the scene of a two story masonry building. The downed firefighter's partner met the volunteer firefighters at the entry door. He said his partner was injured and unable to evacuate the building on his own.

The rescue team gathered their equipment and made entry. Minutes later the firefighters conveyed by radio that they had found the downed firefighter and were initiating a rescue.

Shortly thereafter the firefighters appeared in the doorway with the firefighter. A second evolution got all the volunteers through the training session. The event was a successful one.

Our thanks goes out to the local prison warden for letting us use their building. Also, thank you to professional photographer Chad Wittenberg.

An Innovative Idea

The mandated NFPA 704 placard marking system is a great way that on site hazardous materials are identified.

As a spin off of that methodology, Firefighter Chris McGathy came up with an idea to use a similar system to identify building features all on a mini placard.

In the left upper slot (as you look at it) is the roof and building type, the right upper slot for the FDC and sprinkler system, the lower left slot whether there's a preplan and Knox box, and the lower right slot whether there's a basement and attic. The mini placards will go on the main door into the building.

While it was being developed, Chris put his idea out to the whole department and got some additional ideas from others.

A great innovative idea Firefighter Chris McGathy!

Members

Steve Moody
Joe Haag
Tony Yaghjian
Shane McCoy
Caleb Carson
Caleb Fistler
Chris McGathy
Jack Zimmerman
Mike Rose
Derick Boggs
Bryce Scott
L Jay Geist
Troy Jellison
Coby Spear
Quentin Sage
Sam Aitchison
Sam Wheeler
John Wilson
David Wilson

Scott Van Patten
Brice Denton
Bryce Gann Schwartz
Grant Helferich
Chris Brown
Chris Towner
Brad Sherry
Bill Doan
Zach Floyd
Dakota Huckabee
Chad Whittenberg
Dona Larimer
Bailey Joonas
Landon O'Connor
Jalis Bullock
Jacob Dennett
Richard Hastings
Hailey Jones
Ethan Herrick

Gage Merutka
Grayson Pryce
Dakotah Van Fleet

www.ingramcontent.com/pod-product-compliance
Lightning Source LLC
Chambersburg PA
CBHW070408190526
45169CB00003B/1158